The Treasure Cave

Rosemary Hayes

Illustrated by Ian Newsham

CAMBRIDGE
UNIVERSITY PRESS

Sarah and Marnie were running down the path.
Suddenly, Marnie fell over. She tripped and
fell into an enormous hole. "Help!" she cried.

Sarah knelt on the ground and peered into the
hole. "Marnie!" she shouted. "Are you all right?"

Sarah was very near the edge. Then the ground gave way and *she* fell into the hole, too. She fell a long way, tumbling and bumping, until at last she landed on something soft.

"OUCH!" cried Marnie. "Get off!"

Sarah stood up. "Sorry," she said. "Where are we?"

"Shh," whispered Marnie. "We're in a cave,
I think, and we're not alone. Look over there!"

The light from the hole above them lit up the cave.
At the far end of the cave there were long, dark
shadows. They looked like the shadows of people.

"Who are they?" whispered Marnie.

Very slowly, the girls started to creep forward.

"They look like guards," said Sarah.

"But why are they standing so still?" said Marnie.

"Don't ask me. How should I know?" said Sarah, shivering. She was really scared.

Marnie cleared her throat. "Er . . . excuse me," she said. Her voice echoed in the dark. A bat flew past and made them jump, but the guards didn't move.

Marnie stared and then she laughed. "They're not people at all," she said. "They're just statues!"

"I don't like them. They're really spooky," said Sarah. "Let's get out of here."

But the only way out was through the hole in the roof, and it was far too high to reach. They searched and searched, but they couldn't find another way out.

The girls sat down on a rock beside a small pool. They stared into the water wondering what to do. Then Marnie saw something shiny reflected in the water.

Marnie got up and walked towards the darkest part of the cave. Suddenly she shouted, "Sarah, come over here!"

Sarah ran over to her. She gasped at what she saw.

"It's treasure!" said Sarah. She picked up a diamond bracelet.

They climbed all over the treasure. There were necklaces, earrings, brooches, crowns, belts, buckles and rings. They spent ages trying things on and laughing at each other. Marnie found a golden crown and put it on her head, but it was too big and it kept slipping off. Sarah found the brightest ring and put it on her finger.

The light from the hole grew dimmer.

"It's getting late," said Sarah. "We must get out!"

"Maybe those statues are guarding the entrance," said Marnie. "Let's see if we can get past them."

The girls went back to the statues. Marnie edged past the first guard-statue, but she couldn't help touching it. Sarah followed, but then she stopped. She had seen something.

"Marnie!" said Sarah. "Marnie, wait!" She saw it again. The guard Marnie had touched was moving! Terrified, she watched. The guard shook his head from side to side and yawned.

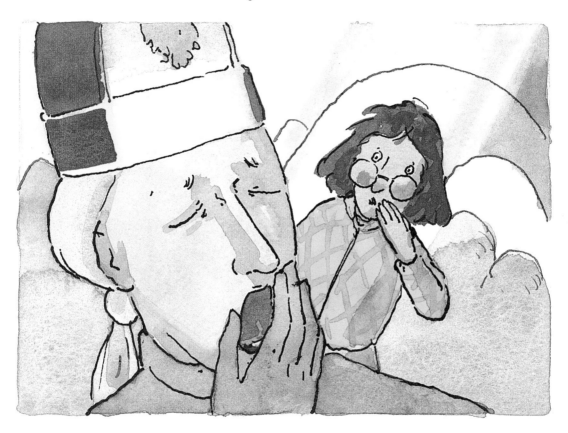

"Marnie!" she called again, "Come back! Get away from them! They're coming alive!" But by now Marnie had touched lots of the guards.

Marnie stopped and looked back. She could hardly believe it.

Every guard that she had touched was starting to move. They were all round her now, blocking her way. But they weren't angry. Instead, they were laughing and shouting and slapping each other on the back.

"Let her out!" shouted Sarah. "Please let her out!"

The first guard looked round and saw Sarah. He walked stiffly towards her. Sarah stepped back.

"Don't be frightened," he said. "By touching us, you have broken the spell. You have saved us."

"What spell?" stuttered Sarah.

The guard explained, "A long time ago, a wicked magician wanted our treasure, so he turned us into statues."

Sarah frowned. "But your treasure's still here," she said.

The guard laughed and his laugh rang round the cave. "Yes," he said, "he wasn't a very clever magician. He turned himself into a statue, too!"

The guard took Sarah by the hand. "If you touch each one of us," he said, "we will all come back to life."

Sarah and Marnie ran round touching all the guards in turn. Then they came to someone who didn't look like a guard. He looked very grumpy and he wore a long cloak.

"Don't touch that one!" yelled the first guard.
"He's the magician." But it was too late. Sarah had
already touched him.

Slowly, the magician came to life. Dust fell from
his cloak and beard and, as he stretched his arms,
something fell on the ground. Sarah bent down
and picked it up. It was the magician's wand.

"Capture him!" cried the first guard. "Capture the magician!" All the guards rushed forward.

"STOP!" thundered the magician, and his voice echoed round the cave like the roar of a lion. "STOP! Or I'll turn you back into stone." The guards stopped. They didn't know what to do.

No-one was looking at Sarah so, very slowly, she crept up behind the magician. She shut her eyes and made a wish. She wished harder than she had ever wished before. Then she touched the magician with the magic wand and ran back to Marnie.

For a moment, nothing happened. Then the magician turned round and stared at the girls.

"Look at his eyes," whispered Marnie. "They're changing! And he's growing lots of hairy legs. And he's shrinking!"

"He's turning into a spider!" said one of the
guards. All at once, everyone started laughing as
they watched the black, hairy spider scuttle across
the floor of the cave and creep into a crack in
the wall. As the spider disappeared, there was
a splintering sound and the wand shattered in
Sarah's hand.

There were shouts and cheers. All the guards started hugging the girls and dancing and jumping and shouting. Marnie was laughing and out of breath. "Please," she said. "Please stop. We must go home."

"But we don't know how to get out," said Sarah.

"Don't worry," said the first guard, "watch us."

Quick as a flash, the guards jumped on each other's shoulders to make a ladder up to the hole in the roof. Sarah climbed up the guards.

Marnie followed her, and soon they were both out of the hole and back on the path.

Marnie rubbed her eyes. "Was that a dream?" she asked.

Sarah frowned. "I don't think so," she said, and she looked at the ring on her finger. It sent out rays of light that made her feel happy.

Marnie peered down into the hole. It was quiet and dark in there now. She called out, but only the echo of her voice came back. Sarah pulled her away. "Come on," she said, "let's go home."

Slowly, Marnie stood up. Then the girls ran off down the path.